THE ENEMY WITHIN

FEAR AS OUR GREATEST OPPONENT

Copyright © 2025

All rights are reserved, and no part of this publication may be reproduced, distributed, or transmitted in any manner, whether through photocopying, recording, or any other electronic or mechanical methods, without the explicit prior written permission of the publisher. This restriction applies to any form or means of reproduction or distribution.

Exceptions to this rule include brief quotations that may be incorporated into critical reviews, as well as certain other noncommercial uses that are allowed by copyright law. Any such usage must adhere to the specified conditions and permissions outlined by the copyright holder.

Book Design by HMDPublishing.com

Dedication

I dedicate this book to my wonderful wife Brianna Wilson, who showed me I can do anything I put my mind to. She showed me not to give up when obstacles are in my path.

I dedicate this book to my mother Elizabeth Sears Wilson for always standing by me and protecting me from everyone who has ever tried to harm me.

I dedicate this book to my third-grade teacher Becky Mowat for always pushing me to strive for more and not giving up on me when I was being hard to deal with.

Contents

Prologue 5
01. A Child's Journey Through Isolation 6
02. Deaf Ears to Universal Cries 12
03. The Breaking Point of Awakening 15
04. Are You Listening? 19
05. Healing the Internal Conflict 21
06. Fear 24
07. Cracking the Door to the Room of Solitude 28
08. Your Inner Power and Moving Forward 32
09. The Worth of a Dollar 38
10. Relationships 41
11. Trust Your Body, It Knows You Best 46
12. Quiet the mind 49
13. The Power of Integration and Moving Forward 52
14. Embracing Change and Transformation 56
15. The Process of Change and Failure 60
16. Conquering Failure in Life 64
17. The Fear of Death and Embracing the Unknown 67
18. Fear as the Catalyst for Growth 72
19. Releasing Your Past and Awaken Your Future 75
A Call to Action 79
The Path Forward - The Journey of Healing 80
About the Author 82

PROLOGUE

Fear is a powerful force. It lingers in the corners of our minds, whispering doubts and planting thoughts of everything that could go wrong. For much of my life, I let fear control my choices, convinced it was something I had to resist or bury. But through my struggles and self-discovery, I had a revelation—fear was never my enemy. It was my guide.

This book is about fear—not as something to be conquered or erased, but as a force to be understood and embraced. Fear can hold us back, yes, but it can also drive us forward, revealing our strengths and guiding us toward growth, healing, and purpose.

The Enemy Within: Fear as Our Greatest Opponent is not just my story; it reflects the human experience. It explores the universal struggle with self-doubt, uncertainty, and the fear of failure. But more than that, it highlights the victory that comes when we learn to see fear for what it truly is—a catalyst for change.

As you turn these pages, I hope you see parts of yourself in my journey. That you begin to question the fears you've been running from and uncover the opportunities they may be concealing. Together, let's redefine fear—not as an enemy, but as an ally.

This is a story of growth. A story of healing. A story of purpose. And it all begins with the courage to face the enemy within.0

CHAPTER 1:
A Child's Journey Through Isolation

This story begins in 1985 when I was born on February 24th at the Queen Elizabeth Hospital in Charlottetown, Prince Edward Island. From a young age, I always felt different from other kids. As the only child in my family, I was naturally needy. I often insisted on getting my way, especially when I wanted my mother to buy something for me.

With both of my parents working, they decided to hire a babysitter, let's call her a woman named Florance. From Monday to Friday, I spent my days with her, arriving in the morning and staying until supper time. Our relationship was difficult—we clashed often. I had a stubborn streak. I didn't like following rules, which led to frequent time-outs. And if things didn't go the way I wanted, I would argue endlessly.

Down the road from Florance's house lived two other kids—one was a girl my age, and the other was a boy a couple of years older. For reasons I couldn't understand, the boy became my first bully. He picked on me because I was smaller and different, turning what should have been fun playtime into rough wrestling matches that always left me hurt. I was an easy target—I didn't know how to fight back, and fear kept me from trying.

As time passed, my fear only grew. I told my mother about the bullying, and she spoke to his parents, but it didn't stop. Then came my first day of school. I was nervous and scared, unprepared to be around so many other children. I worried that if I said the wrong thing, they would laugh at me. In class, I struggled with my schoolwork. Reading frustrated me, and I lost interest quickly. My teacher eventually decided that I would benefit more from spending recess outside playing instead of trying to focus on lessons that overwhelmed me. But even then, my mind drifted, and I consistently struggled to engage.

Grade one was a fight from start to finish. After school, getting me to do homework was a battle. I had trouble learning, staying focused, and keeping up with my classmates. Eventually, my teacher recommended that I repeat the first grade. That was my first real experience with failure, and it hit me hard. It shook my self-esteem and set me on a downward path that affected my emotional growth.

Instead of repeating the first grade a second time, the school decided to move me ahead because "no kid gets left behind." They suspected I had ADD, so my parents took me to a specialist. The experience was strange—he had me hitting dummies with a plastic bat. I'm not sure how he reached a diagnosis, but my parents eventually tried to put me on medication. I refused, and after some debate, they agreed I shouldn't be on pills. That summer is mostly a blur—I blocked out much of it.

When second grade started, my new teacher wasn't new. It was the same teacher, and this year, she didn't seem to like me. She soon labelled me a troublemaker and often kept me inside during recess, forcing me to complete assignments I struggled to understand. Doubts about my abilities took root. I found it harder and harder to connect with other children, constantly second-guessing myself. I was terrified of making any mistakes in front of my classmates. My confidence slowly crumbled until, eventually, I gave up completely.

That year, for my birthday, my mother rented a bowling alley, and we had a pizza party with cake. But out of nowhere, I became violently ill and started vomiting. When my mother took me to the doctor, we found out I was a carrier of strep throat. I had been unknowingly carrying the illness for some time. Now, I had no choice but to take medication, and I was forced to stay indoors for the winter instead of playing outside—away from the bullies but stuck with schoolwork.

Winter was brutal. I had to do schoolwork at lunchtime, spending hours struggling through assignments, often in tears.

When I was able to return outdoors for recess, a new kid joined the class. He quickly became another bully, targeting me every day. Once again, I found myself in a cycle of fear. My parents stepped in and spoke with the school, but nothing changed. I dreaded going to school and begged my mother and father to keep me home, but I had no choice—I had to face it.

But despite everything, I somehow passed. My teacher, aware of my challenges, allowed me to move on to the next grade. However, I didn't feel like I had earned it. My self-esteem was at an all-time low, and I became more withdrawn. School had become a battlefield, and I was losing every fight.

That summer, I tried learning a sport. I struggled with T-ball because I didn't have the basics down. I just wanted to play, but without the skills, I stuck out as an outsider. Even though I loved sports, I was never good at them—my mind was too cluttered with fear and self-doubt. I was always afraid of being inadequate. While I enjoyed hitting the ball, the constant anxiety of messing up kept me from fully embracing the game.

Grade three came around, and although my struggles continued, I had a teacher who, despite having little patience for me, genuinely wanted me to succeed. She challenged me in ways no other teacher had. Unknown to me, she would become one of my inspirations for this book later in life. Our relationship was tense—I spent a lot of time in the office after arguing with her—but deep down, I respected her for pushing me to do better.

At this point, I became a bully myself. I'm not sure why I chose this student, but I did. I hated myself for it afterward and later apologized to him. At that moment, I realized I wasn't much different from those who had tormented me. My reputation as the "problem child" spread among other parents, and I was rarely in class—either skipping or too lost in my thoughts to pay attention.

My struggles continued, but in grade four, I met new kids and hoped I could finally fit in. Even then, friendships weren't always easy. My bully was getting stronger, and I felt more isolated than ever. The battlefield remained, and I started noticing how much it had affected my mental health. Reluctantly, I dragged myself through eight more tedious years of this journey I learned to know as my life.

As I moved from adolescence into adulthood, the patterns of isolation and confusion followed me into my relationships. Growing up, I had never built strong emotional connections, so when it came time to navigate relationships, I was lost. I didn't know how to be a boyfriend, nor did I understand what a healthy relationship looked like. Conversations felt unnatural because I wasn't used to truly engaging with people. I had always been alone.

One relationship stands out particularly. I was dating a girl, and during a casual conversation, I used the word "tacky." I thought it was a compliment, but it wasn't. I didn't realize until later that I had insulted her, and the damage was done. I apologized, but I didn't understand why I wasn't more concerned about what had gone wrong. Back then, I drifted through life without any effort–the effort to better myself, my relationships, or even my connection with my parents.

I lacked the tools to process my emotions or healthily express them. My immaturity kept me from building lasting relationships, and I could never seem to maintain one. They either fell apart because I wasn't emotionally present, or I withdrew the first moment I felt insecure. It was an endless cycle that repeated itself. Looking back, I see it for what it was—trauma at work. Fear and avoidance drove me to sabotage what could have been meaningful relationships.

The turning point came when I started working as a carpenter's helper. The job was miserable. I constantly clashed with the boss's brother-in-law, who communicated by yelling, making me feel small and insignificant. By the second summer, I had built a little more confidence, but the tension with my girlfriend's family—also my coworkers—only grew. I vented my frustrations to her, but she didn't want to hear it. I didn't know how to handle stress in a relationship. We argued, and one day, I found myself yelling at her. We got out of the car, faced each other, and suddenly realized how ridiculous we were being. For a moment, it felt like a breakthrough, a glimpse of maturity—but it didn't last. Eventually, we broke up, and once again, I was left to deal with the consequences of my inability to communicate and connect.

I began to understand why my relationships kept falling apart. I wasn't emotionally equipped to handle the vulnerability that came with closeness. I didn't know how to trust others because I had never trusted myself. My fear of rejection and failure kept people at arm's length, and when things got difficult, I would retreat or push them away. I didn't know how to ask for help or open up about my fears. The idea of "fixing" myself had never felt real or necessary; I was too caught up in a cycle of self-sabotage.

I had always wanted to work in radio, but my confidence had been shattered after being told I was wasting my time when I applied for a broadcasting course. That rejection hit me hard, and I no longer had the discipline to chase my dreams. Eventually, I decided to pursue a career—partly because I needed something to focus on. So, I pivoted to the course my guidance counsellor had recommended. After a period of indecision, I found myself enrolled in a course designed to help people with intellectual disabilities. It was an odd experience at first. I was the only guy in the class, surrounded by women, and I felt awkward and out of place. The course itself wasn't the problem—it was me. I scuffled with communication, understanding boundaries, and expressing myself. But this job, working with people who had intellectual disabilities, gave me a sense of purpose.

Still, I wasn't fully present. I was battling my demons. I had a hidden addiction to marijuana that I had kept secret for a long time. Eventually, I confided in my teacher, and she sent me to my first NA meeting. It was a peculiar encounter, one that I never fully embraced. I attended a retreat, but before long, I veered off track. I didn't put in the effort to truly heal, to understand the roots of my addiction, or to take responsibility for my actions. I gave up too quickly, as I had done so many times before.

Yet, at the same time, my physical health became a central focus. I committed to working out and took pride in completing the P90X Program. The results were visible, and for the first time in my life, I felt a sense of control over something. It gave me confidence, yet the internal work remained unfinished. I still struggled with communication, especially with women. Shyness made every interaction feel like an uphill battle. I often felt like an outsider in my own life, unsure of how to be fully present in a relationship.

It wasn't until later, through deeper reflection, that I uncovered the root of my problems. My relationships mirrored the unresolved trauma I carried from childhood—the fear of rejection, the lack of communication skills, and the emotional distance. I had never acquired how to engage in meaningful connections because I grew up in an environment of isolation, fear, and silence. I didn't know how to build relationships, so I avoided them altogether. This fear wasn't limited to personal connections; it spilled into every aspect of my life. I was afraid of failure, afraid of vulnerability and judgment.

As I grew older, I came to an essential realization: the mind and body are deeply connected. If the mind remains wounded, the body will reflect that imbalance. My physical struggles—the frequent exhaustion and the times I felt incapable of functioning—were all signals from my body urging me to slow down. But I ignored those warnings, numbing myself with alcohol, drugs, and unhealthy habits. My body was begging me to stop, yet I refused to listen. It wasn't until much later, when I embraced self-awareness and self-care that I finally tuned in to what my body and mind had been trying to tell me all along.

CHAPTER 2:
DEAF EARS TO UNIVERSAL CRIES

My mother and father just arrived at the hospital. My father looked at me and said, "Boy, you're lucky to be alive because not too many people survive something like that. Even the doctor told me you should be paralyzed. The way you fell, your spine should have snapped in half."

It was wintertime in 2009. I had fallen twenty-seven feet from a chair lift at a ski resort. Someone had fallen from the chair behind me, jerking the cable line and the seat. I was leaning forward with the T-bar elevated, which forced me off. I plummeted to the ground and passed out midair. I woke up in the snow, surrounded by a crowd of people. I was immediately rushed to the hospital for X-rays and medical attention. Ironically, I had been lifting the T-bar to reposition my snowboard because years prior, I had my skull cracked open from an accident of being hit in the head with a chair lift. I never did have luck on the hill.

That moment laying in the hospital bed should have been my awakening to spirituality, though I didn't recognize it at the time. Something—some force—stopped me from dying that day. I didn't know what it was. All I knew was that it had saved me. I should have paid attention to that moment, but I didn't. Instead, I kept pushing my luck, making reckless decisions the entire time.

Then came the winter of 2010, and I made another one. I had just left a Christmas party, and once again, I took a risk by driving when I shouldn't have. I fell asleep at the wheel, and the next thing I knew, I was crashing into a telephone pole. Once again, I don't know how I survived, but I did. My knee took the worst of it, badly chipped and damaged. When I climbed out of the vehicle, I could still walk. It wasn't until the shock wore off that I realized I couldn't put any pressure on that leg. And yet, I had survived.

By 2015, I had started working at a Canadian refinery plant for a company based out of Texas. The company assured us the air was safe, insisting no hazardous chemicals were on the job site. But, of course, they lied. There were chemicals in the air, and my monitor kept going off. Suddenly, I felt a sharp, unbearable pain in my chest. I climbed into the truck with my foreman, but the damage was already done. The H2S gas had entered my system. By the time we reached the medic shack, my eyes burned so badly it felt like acid was being poured into them, and my lungs were on fire. It was the worst pain I had ever felt. They airlifted me to the hospital—three hours away by car but only a half-hour by helicopter. That experience should have been another warning, but I still didn't learn.

Then came 2019. I was driving home after a gruelling 14-hour shift. It was winter, and as we rounded a curve near Dome Creek, we lost control of the vehicle. A truck was stopped ahead of us—we should have slammed right into it. But somehow, we stopped just a foot away. I stepped out, completely unharmed. Another close call. Another sign completely missed.

These near-death experiences, I now realize, were the Universe's way of trying to wake me up. It was as if my Guides were screaming, "You're not listening!". I kept pushing through my trauma, numbing the pain with distractions. I worked in an industry where I was treated as nothing more than a number—a tool to be used and discarded. It was a place where I was yelled at, belittled, and expected to accept the abuse. And I did because that's what I had always done. But deep down, I had reached my limit. The truth is…I had been at my limit for a long time, but it took me years to recognize the real cause of my mistakes—my denial to heal from past trauma.

For years, I ignored my pain, buried it, and kept moving forward without addressing the wounds inside me. I worked hard to drown out the discomfort. I wasn't truly paying attention. These experiences were not just accidents or coincidences; they were lessons. They were messages I had been refusing to acknowledge.

Fear and unresolved trauma clouded my judgment and once again impacted my relationships. Looking back, I now understand that these messages were attempts to push me toward change, urging me to confront my past and heal. If I had listened earlier, I could have avoided a lot of suffering—but I didn't. Instead, I brushed everything off, convincing myself it didn't matter. But it did. Everything that happens, especially the painful moments, holds meaning.

CHAPTER 3
THE BREAKING POINT OF AWAKENING

In August 2021, after a gruelling 10-day work week, I found myself on the road, working just outside of High Level, Alberta. I was exhausted but eager to get home to my family when an unexpected call from Sturgeon Staffing came through. The name didn't ring a bell, so I let it go to voicemail. But the message I received changed everything.

The hospital informed me that my mother's condition had taken a drastic turn for the worse. Her kidneys were failing due to a septic kidney stone. My mother was going to die.

By the time I finally made it home, it was already too late to visit her that night, so I decided to go first thing in the morning. What I found was heartbreaking—my mother lay unconscious, surrounded by machines, her body frail and motionless. There was no clear indication of what would happen next. The doctors explained that she needed an urgent surgical procedure to insert a stent in her kidney. She was airlifted to another hospital, and I could do nothing but wait anxiously for an update.

That afternoon, I got the call I had been praying for—the surgery was successful, and she was stable. A wave of relief washed over me.

But it was short-lived.

At 12:30 AM, the same nurse called again. This time, the news was devastating. My mother's condition had rapidly deteriorated, and I needed to get to her as soon as possible.

I rushed to the hospital in Edmonton, suited up in full protective gear, and stepped into her room, where she lay in unbearable discomfort. Guilt weighed heavily on me as I sat beside her, whispering apologies for the argument we had before I left.

I wanted her to know that I loved her.

I needed her to know that I was sorry.

A doctor entered the room, his expression solemn. He looked at me and quietly said what I had been dreading—my mother didn't have much time left.

I stayed with her for hours, pleading with God to spare her, hoping against hope that she would somehow pull through. Watching her slip away while being powerless to stop it was the most excruciating experience of my life.

After eight long hours, the nurse returned and softly told me it was time. With the machines being turned off and in the stillness of the room, I watched helplessly as my mother took her last breath. She passed peacefully in her sleep.

Losing my mother was a pain unlike anything I had ever known. I was consumed by grief, anger, and confusion. I blamed everyone and everything, even my ex-girlfriend, despite knowing that none of it was her fault. I was angry at the world, at the unfairness of it all. I couldn't understand why this had to happen or why I didn't get more time with her.

Even as I wrote this book almost four years later, I will always acknowledge this as the darkest time of my life. As far as I knew, at that point in life, I was officially alone.

Desperate for answers to make sense of my grief, I soon turned to conversations with a few coworkers—people who adamantly refused the COVID-19 vaccine. They introduced me to conspiracy theories, and soon, I found myself spiralling into an endless search for explanations that might ease the chaos in my mind. I became fixated. But this fear-driven thinking was just a distraction—an escape from confronting the deeper pain of losing my mother.

Then, something life-changing happened. I met someone who introduced me to the teachings of Dolores Cannon. Chapter after chapter, I became fixated. As I immersed myself in her books, I saw life through an entirely new lens. I realized that death wasn't something to fear—it was simply a transition, a natural step in our existence. Our physical lives are temporary, a brief experience, and death is not an ending but a return home to where we truly belong.

What I hadn't understood before was that we are not of this world—we come here to learn, to evolve, and to grow. Life is not about conforming to the structures that society imposes on us; it's about discovering our true selves. Too many people move through life on autopilot, never questioning their purpose, never engaging in the deep self-reflection required to wake up to their full potential.

Through this awakening, I realized that I had to release my attachment to my mother's passing. Holding onto my grief kept her spirit tied to this world, preventing her from moving forward. Mourning becomes an anchor and is a way of refusing to let go. True love is about allowing our loved ones the freedom to continue their journey beyond this life.

This is the understanding we all need to reach—that it's not the end that defines us, but what we do with the time we are given. Embrace the unexpected turns, the challenges, and the painful lessons because each experience shapes you into a stronger, more self-aware version of yourself.

The more we embrace life's journey, the more we recognize that every moment presents an opportunity to grow, to release fear, and to shed outdated beliefs that no longer serve us. Every struggle is a chance to break free from limitations, and every victory is simply a reminder of our resilience. We are capable of far more than we often allow ourselves to believe.

If you can learn to accept life's uncertainty, remain present, and trust the path as it unfolds, you will find a deep sense of peace and fulfillment that will sustain you through even the hardest times. You are never truly alone—your loved ones, unseen guides, and the very essence of life walk beside you, supporting you every step of the way.

So, stop waiting for the perfect moment. Stop waiting for everything to align before you act. The time to embrace the journey is now. Every step you take brings you closer to where you are meant to be. Trust yourself. Trust the process. Every experience—good or bad—has a purpose in shaping your story, a story filled with meaning, growth, and limitless possibilities.

Letting go of the past, releasing fear, and surrendering control is not about giving up—it's about stepping into the natural flow of life. It's about recognizing that every moment. Every experience guides you toward something greater. When we release what no longer serves us, we create space for new opportunities, transformation, and peace.

You are exactly where you need to be. Your journey is unfolding as it should. Trust it. Allow it to lead you forward. Your subconscious will never steer you wrong.

Chapter 4

Are You Listening?

Every day, our bodies communicate with us, but we often ignore the signals. We fail to see that pain, illness, and even the smallest discomforts are messages telling us to slow down, to let go, and to forgive ourselves. It's not just physical pain—sometimes it's emotional or mental. These lingering feelings, whether from an argument, stress at work, or the weight of failure, are signs of our bodies. They are indicators trying to show us what we need to release and what still needs healing.

Many of us dismiss these warnings, which is why we continue making the same mistakes and enduring the same struggles. The truth is our ego gets in the way. We convince ourselves we need to push harder, to disregard the pain. However, in all reality, the more we ignore it, the more damage it causes in the long run. The ringing in your ears, the exhaustion, the aches—these are not random. They are your body, your spirit, and your inner self trying to communicate with you. And you need to listen.

Our energy is powerful; it shapes the world around us. When you operate from a place of love, compassion, and understanding, you attract that same energy in return. It doesn't matter if someone cuts you off in traffic or a loved one is upset with you. They still deserve love—just as much as you do. We are all connected, both energetically and spiritually. When we embrace this truth, we create a ripple effect of healing that extends far beyond ourselves.

When you release the trauma that has held you back, your true healing begins. When you heal, your body, mind, and soul start working in harmony. You stop fighting yourself. You stop allowing the past to dictate your present, and instead, you begin shaping the future you deserve.

For so long, I blamed others for my failures. I let negativity and other people's opinions control my life. I convinced myself that I was incapable of success. But the truth is, it was me all along. I was the one standing in my way. I allowed fear—fear of failure, fear of judgment—to hold me back.

Now, I see things differently. Success isn't about money or status—it's about growth, self-love, and spiritual awakening. When you believe in yourself and find the courage to trust your journey, the universe starts opening doors for you. That's when you truly grasp the power of manifestation and the law of attraction. The life you desire is already within reach. All you need to do is take the step and believe you deserve it.

That's what I want this book to be—a reminder that we are not lost. We just haven't yet found the right path. But with time and the courage to heal, you will find your way. You will discover peace. Life is a school. It is a place where we are meant to learn, grow, and support one another. Our purpose is not merely to exist but to thrive—to bring balance, understanding, and love into the world. It's not about accumulating wealth; it's about lifting each other to a higher vibration. It's about being present for one another. This is the true essence of life.

CHAPTER 3:
HEALING THE INTERNAL CONFLICT

You are not lost. You are exactly where you need to be. Now, it's time to listen to the messages your body and soul have sent to you all along. Take a step forward. Heal. Grow. And create something meaningful—not just for yourself but for the world.

By unchaining yourself, you allow your energy to flow freely, affecting those around you. You cultivate a warm, welcoming space where others feel safe to be themselves. When you embrace vulnerability and trust in yourself and the process, you begin the process to shift your energy. The energy you emit is felt by those around you. And, in turn, it inspires them to elevate their own. This is how we cultivate harmony and peace. You are no longer just living for yourself—you are uplifting others, and your energy becomes a force for healing.

Trusting yourself and trusting the journey you're on is essential. Life may lead you down roads that seem uncertain or difficult, and some experiences will undoubtedly be painful. But every single one, whether joyful or challenging, holds significance. They are all lessons meant to teach and shape you. Once you begin to absorb these lessons, your growth begins. And with growth comes spiritual awakening. Your true purpose starts to emerge, and you gain a deeper understanding of everything you've endured.

As your spiritual awakening deepens, so does your ability to heal. Healing your inner child—the part that still carries pain from your past—allows you to reclaim your wholeness. You begin to feel at peace with yourself, aligned with your spirit. You realize that you are not separate from those around you. We are all connected to the same source, the energy that holds the universe together. We are not isolated beings but part of a greater, interconnected existence.

The struggles you face in this life are not random obstacles; they are stepping stones leading you to your true purpose. It may not always be clear at that moment, but once you gain insight, you'll recognize how every challenge presented played a critical role in guiding you toward your destiny. You'll understand that these hardships were placed in your path to strengthen you. To teach you trust, love, and growth.

When you discover your purpose, that's when transformation begins. You start building something meaningful—something abundant, not just for yourself but for those around you. You create a life ingrained in growth, love, compassion, and harmony. Instead of chasing material wealth or status, you will begin seeking joy, connection, and fulfillment. Your focus shifts to positivity. You affirm yourself, support those in need, and radiate kindness to everyone you encounter.

As you move forward on this journey, remember that everything is alive. Your body, thoughts, and actions—all of them are expressions of energy. The earth, the food you consume, the money you earn—are all extensions of the energy that flows through everything. We are not separate from it. We are a part of it. So, communicate with your body. Listen to it. Care for it with love and respect. Extend that same love to those around you. Acknowledge the needs of others, honour nature, and respect the balance of all living things. Everything is connected.

Be courageous. Don't fear what's ahead—embrace the opportunities that await you. By opening yourself up and raising your energy, you subconsciously create space for new experiences, personal growth, and new beginnings. Don't let fear or doubt hold you back. You've already learned that unhealed pain can weigh you down, but now, it's time to move forward. Open your mind, prepare for what's to come, and trust that every door you open leads you to a higher level of being.

What life has taught me is that we cannot blame others for the challenges we face. True change comes from looking inward—understanding the choices we've made, the energy we've put into the world, and what we have attracted into our lives. Pain is powerful, and if we allow it, it can control us. It can keep us from success, from the loving relationships we long for, and from the abundance that is our birthright.

For me, trauma was the force that kept me stuck. I allowed it to control me. But it wasn't until I realized that I had played a role in attracting it into my life that I truly understood the depth of my journey. I drew these painful experiences toward me because of the energy I carried—because I didn't believe in myself. The energy I put out into the world shaped my reality. That's the hard truth: We are the architects of our own lives. We shape the environment we live in through our thoughts, beliefs, and actions.

Confidence is the key to breaking free from the cycle of trauma. Courage is what keeps you moving forward, even when the road ahead is uncertain. Love is the force that connects you to everyone and everything. It is the universal language, and when you act from a place of love, you align yourself with the natural flow of the universe.

As you grow, you'll realize that every challenge, every hardship, and every painful moment is an opportunity to align with your higher purpose. Everything you've endured has led you here—to a life of love, peace, and spiritual clarity. Embrace this journey. Understand that your trauma does not define you; your response to it does. And when you choose love, when you choose healing, you will discover the life that was always meant for you.

CHAPTER 6

FEAR

Fear will always be a formidable opponent. It lingers in the back of your mind, whispering doubts, planting seeds of uncertainty. *What if this doesn't work? What if they laugh at me? What if I get fired? What if I don't make enough money this week?* Do you see the pattern? These thoughts, these fears, are not just fleeting doubts—they are powerful forces. They create cycles of negativity, and at their core, they stem from self-doubt. We constantly talk ourselves into fear without even realizing it.

Once you release fear—fear of change, fear of being alone, fear of failure—you open yourself to the possibilities ahead. You begin to understand that your worth is not tied to your job, material possessions, or even relationships. Your worth is innate. You are valuable simply because you exist. The moment you recognize your value, you will start to attract the people, situations, and opportunities that align with your true self.

Overcoming this fear is one of life's greatest challenges: the mind's ability to control our emotions and, ultimately, shape our reality. When you fixate on what scares you—failure, rejection, or loss—you give it power. You feel that fear, fueling it, feeding it energy, and in doing so, you amplify its presence. It's like turning on a spotlight that highlights everything you are afraid of, allowing those same fears to take form in your life.

Think about it: when you focus on what you don't want, that's often exactly what you get. It's a destructive cycle. If you constantly worry about money, for example, the universe responds to that energy of worry by bringing more financial stress into your life. The more you focus on lack or limitation, the more you reinforce those feelings, and in turn, they manifest as your reality.

The truth is fear is an illusion. It is a mental construct designed to protect you, but in most cases, it is unnecessary. The things we fear rarely come to pass, and even when they do, we have the strength and resilience to overcome them. Fear only holds power if we give it power. Once we recognize this, we stop living in fear and start embracing life with boldness, courage, and excitement—knowing that we can achieve greatness.

The key to breaking this cycle is to shift your focus. You must become aware of when fear is creeping in and make a conscious choice to redirect your energy. Instead of asking, *what if I fail? Ask yourself, What if this works? Instead of thinking, what if I get rejected? Replace it with, what if I succeed beyond my wildest dreams?* The very moment you shift from fear-based thinking into possibility-based thinking, you automatically generate a new energy. You give life to something different—something positive, hopeful, and empowering.

It's important to understand that fear does not suddenly rise out of nothing; it is shaped by our thoughts, beliefs, and past experiences. Fear is often a reflection of stories we tell ourselves about what is possible and what is not. These stories stem from past trauma, disappointments, or societal conditioning—but they are not the truth. They are simply the narratives we have chosen to accept.

Once you recognize that you have the power to rewrite these narratives, fear loses its grip on you. You can choose to believe in your worth, in your ability to succeed, and in your power to create the life you desire. Fear only controls you if you allow it to. When you decide to confront your fears rather than avoid them, you begin transforming them into opportunities for growth.

One powerful tool for overcoming fear is visualization. Instead of imagining the worst-case scenario, picture the best. See yourself succeeding, accomplishing your goals, and thriving in every aspect of your life. The more vividly you visualize this, the more real it becomes in your mind. Your brain does not distinguish between a detailed visualization and reality, so when you consistently envision success, your body and energy begin to align with that vision.

Another essential step in overcoming fear is to act—even when you're scared. Fear thrives on hesitation. It feeds on procrastination and avoidance. But when you take even one small step forward, despite your fear, you disrupt the cycle. Every action, no matter how small, weakens fear's grip. You will find that the more you act, the more your confidence grows. And as confidence builds, fear diminishes, replaced by courage and clarity.

Ask yourself: What can I do to make myself happy? What can I do to show myself love and compassion? The answers may surprise you. A goal, an idea, or a dream you've been neglecting might come to mind. Hold on to that thought. Nurture it. Believe in it. Pour love and intention into it. Trust the process and watch as it unfolds into something meaningful.

You have the power to shape your reality with your thoughts and energy. Fear is not something to avoid; it is something to acknowledge, understand, and transform. By shifting your mindset, taking action, and trusting the process, you can rewrite your story and create a life that reflects your deepest desires.

The choice is always yours. If you want to change your life, you must start by transforming yourself. And that transformation begins with self-belief, love, and a commitment to your happiness.

Remember, you are not alone in this. Everyone faces fear, but not everyone chooses to move through it. When you decide to rise above fear, you unlock a world of possibilities—possibilities that lead to success, love, and abundance. The choice is yours. Choose courage over fear. Choose growth over stagnation. And watch as life unfolds in ways you never imagined possible.

So, when fear arises—and it will—remember that it is simply a signal. It is an invitation to grow, to learn, and to evolve. It is not a roadblock; it is a stepping stone. Every time you face your fear, you strengthen your ability to shape the life you desire. Acknowledge fear as a companion on your journey, but do not let it steer the ship. You are the captain of your destiny—fear is simply a passenger.

CHAPTER 7
Cracking the Door to the Room of Solitude

How many of us are truly afraid to be alone with our thoughts? I think, on some level, we all experience this fear. When I first embarked on this solo retreat, the idea of being alone with nothing but my thoughts was unsettling. The silence felt overwhelming, and I worried I wouldn't be able to handle it. I thought I would cave that the discomfort of being by myself—without distractions like my phone, the internet, or social media—would be too much to bear. It felt like an impossible challenge.

But to my surprise, I didn't cave at all. I stayed committed to the purpose of the retreat and learned to embrace the silence.

At first, it wasn't easy. Every part of me wanted to reach for something—anything—to break the quiet. But I resisted, reminding myself that the goal of this retreat was to find peace within myself and the stillness around me. It's easy to assume we can't handle silence, but once I allowed myself to just be, I realized I was far more capable than I had given myself credit for.

By the end of day one, I felt proud of myself. I had faced the discomfort of solitude, and instead of running from it, I stayed present with my thoughts and emotions. Even more surprising was what I accomplished. One of the most unexpected moments was when I re-taught myself how to build a fire. There was something grounding about watching the flames rise, casting a warm orange glow. It soothed me in a way I hadn't anticipated—something so simple yet deeply fulfilling.

This retreat also became a journey of rediscovering parts of myself I hadn't connected with in years. I hadn't written like this in a long time. The last time I poured my thoughts onto paper with this level of passion and reflection was back in sixth grade when I used to create stories from my imagination. That feeling of writing without restriction or judgment—simply letting my thoughts flow freely—was something I hadn't experienced in ages. I was amazed at how liberating it felt to put my emotions into words, allowing each thought to spill onto the page without hesitation.

One of the most powerful things about journaling is the release it provides. In today's fast-paced world, we often forget that we can express our thoughts on paper before speaking them aloud. How often do we find ourselves caught up in gossip, miscommunication, or awkward situations simply because we don't take the time to process our emotions first? Writing gives us the space to quiet the noise, reflect without external influences, and understand our emotions without judgment.

One of the most rewarding aspects of this retreat was how it pushed me to do the inner work. It challenged me to step beyond my comfort zone and face my fears head-on. Today, for the very first time, I tried snowshoeing. I had no idea how intense the workout would be! With every step, I felt the muscles in my legs working. And it wasn't just my legs—I could feel the effort in my core as well. The deeper I moved into the snow, the more I felt my body being tested. But in that challenge, I uncovered something about myself: I am stronger and more capable than I ever realized.

Sometimes, we don't realize what we're capable of until we push ourselves beyond our comfort zone. It all starts with the right mindset. The biggest lesson I've learned so far is that if I overanalyze, I overthink. If I overthink, I become insecure. And when I become insecure, I create anxiety. From there, anxiety feeds into fear. And when we're operating from fear, it's nearly impossible to make any meaningful progress.

But when we let go of those fears—when we clear our minds and focus—we can create anything we desire.

This realization has been life-changing for me. It's so easy to get caught in negative thought patterns to spiral into overthinking, insecurity, and anxiety. But when we learn to quiet our minds and direct our energy with intention, we take control of our reality instead of allowing our thoughts to control us.

The power of silence has also been a key part of my journey. We often view silence as something to fear—something that makes us feel uncomfortable or exposed. But silence is one of the most valuable tools we have. When we allow ourselves to be alone with our thoughts, we create space to reconnect with who we truly are. In silence, we block out distractions and return to our essence.

Our egos thrive on noise. They seek distractions and use them to pull us away from what truly matters. But when we surrender to silence, we drown out the ego's interference. We stop listening to the voices in our heads that tell us we're not good enough, that we're incapable, and that we need to compare ourselves to others. Silence gives us clarity, helping us focus on our true path without interference.

This retreat has also reinforced the importance of being present in the moment. In business, it's easy to get caught in the pressure to constantly hustle, to prove ourselves, to chase success at all costs. But success isn't about endlessly pushing ourselves to the brink. It's about trusting the process, being present, and allowing opportunities to unfold as we do the work—without fear or doubt.

As a QHHT practitioner, I'm learning that I don't need to chase clients. I need to trust that they will find me when the time is right. The more we try to force something to happen, the more we create resistance. The key is to release the need for control and allow things to unfold as they are meant to. It's not about success or failure—it's about being in alignment with our purpose and trusting the timing of our lives.

Too often, we focus on what we lack—what we don't have, what we haven't yet achieved, or where we believe we're falling short. However, focusing on scarcity only reinforces feelings of lack. The true path to success and fulfillment is shifting our focus toward abundance. When we appreciate what we have, acknowledge what's working, and recognize the progress we've already made, we invite more of the same into our lives.

Our thoughts hold immense power. They shape our reality and influence every outcome we experience.

If we go to bed with our minds full of worries, doubts, or anxieties, those thoughts will likely shape our dreams. But if we clear our minds before we sleep, we invite peace. Being alone with our thoughts is a form of self-care—a way to reconnect with our inner calm. When we stop filling our lives with distractions and allow our minds to rest, we create space to heal and grow.

This retreat has made me realize just how much we depend on external distractions—especially technology. Our phones, social media, and constant connection to the outside world have ironically disconnected us more than ever. We've become obsessed with staying plugged into the digital world, yet in the process, we've lost touch with ourselves. We rely on social media for validation, for gaining followers, and for growing our businesses. But this endless pursuit of comparison and approval has only created an environment where our egos take control.

What would happen if all of that disappeared? If the technology we depend on—our phones, social media, the internet—were to crash for good, how would we exist? How would we adapt? The plot thickens, doesn't it?

We have become so reliant on technology that we've forgotten how to truly thrive without it. But in silence, in solitude, we can rediscover our true selves. The question is: Are we ready to step away from the distractions and embrace the freedom that comes with being fully present with our own thoughts?

Chapter 8:
Your Inner Power and Moving Forward

You have the power within you to connect with your true self, find inner peace, and love yourself unconditionally. This is a gift—the ability to forgive not just others but yourself. As you grow and evolve, your fears begin to lose their grip, and pain no longer defines you. Instead of fearing life's challenges, you learn to see them as lessons, each teaching you something valuable. This is personal growth—shaping the life you want and the valuable connections you are worthy of.

Do not let fear hold you back. Take chances. Stepping beyond the fear that has shadowed you for so long is already a victory. We've all carried doubt, trauma, and uncertainty, but the real strength lies in how we confront them. Use those experiences as fuel for your progress. Let them push you toward helping others. Share your story with those who are struggling—whether they battle self-doubt, impostor syndrome, bullying, or the fear of failure.

We all carry wounds from the past, but they don't have to define us. If we choose to learn from them, they can become a source of strength. You are capable, guided, and loved—nothing can take that from you. On the hard days, look in the mirror and remind yourself: I love you. I understand myself. It took time to get here, but I embrace who I am now. There is no turning back. When you accept your past and take the lessons forward, you release its hold on you.

It's time to release the past and step into something meaningful—something you can be proud of. That's exactly what I'm doing. I'm writing this book for everyone who has ever felt beaten down, misunderstood, or different. If you struggle with communication, feel out of sync with others, or don't fit into the mold, know this: being different is a strength. It takes courage to stand out, but it means you see the world in a way others don't. Your creativity, perspective, and vision set you apart. You are not limited by what others believe—you can achieve more than you ever imagined.

Start small. Take one small step each day to improve by just 1%. Over time, these small efforts will build upon each other, leading to profound change. You can achieve anything if you believe in yourself. Even when you don't see it, you inspire others. You and I have something in common—we have both faced obstacles, yet we continue to rise. The ability to understand pain is a gift because it teaches us resilience and helps us appreciate our journey.

I am proud of you, even if we've never met. We are both on a journey of growth, and you should hold your head high, recognizing all that you've accomplished. Don't let anyone diminish that. Trust yourself, listen to your inner voice, and let it guide you in the right direction. Stay humble, and everything will fall into place.

No one can take away your power. You are unstoppable, fueled by a mindset that refuses to accept failure. You have goals, you set boundaries, and you're stepping away from toxic people who no longer add value to your life. Every effort you make to improve yourself brings you closer to success—not just in wealth, but in happiness and fulfillment.

Life will always test us in different ways. Whether we acknowledge it or not, it's like a video game—each challenge appears in various forms, some minor, some overwhelming. But every challenge serves a purpose: to push us, strengthen us, and offer opportunities to rise above. There will be moments when obstacles feel relentless, but each one is designed to teach you invaluable.

The key is not to fear challenges. Don't fear failure, difficulty, or the unknown. Every time you face adversity, you gain wisdom. Every lesson fuels your growth. This process is ongoing, and each step toward becoming a stronger version of yourself is a victory. Life may test you, but it also rewards those who embrace its lessons.

So, welcome the discomfort, face the challenges, and absorb the wisdom they bring. The journey may not always be easy, but with each hurdle you overcome, you move closer to the person you are meant to be—strong, capable, and ready to accomplish anything. Keep pushing forward because you are limitless.

What we resist, we often attract. What we desire, we attract as well. It sounds like a paradox, but it's real. The energy we release into the world—whether we realize it or not—returns to us. The biggest challenge in life is understanding that we are responsible for shaping our reality. We create our struggles, even when we don't recognize them. We tell ourselves things happen randomly or that they're beyond our control. But in truth, our energy, mindset, and unresolved pain are what set these events into motion.

Whether you believe it or not, the truth is that everything I've endured in life didn't happen because the universe was against me. It happened because I was repaying a debt—a debt I created, not in this life, but in a past one. This concept can be hard to accept, but once you understand it, everything begins to make sense. Many of us fail to see how past actions, not just in this lifetime but in previous experiences, influence the path we walk today.

This realization didn't come easily. It took me well into adulthood to understand. I kept believing life was happening to me, but in truth, I was attracting experiences that reflected the pain and fears I hadn't addressed. We often assume we're right in situations, but growth isn't about being right—it's about understanding. Our ego rushes to defend us, insisting we're justified, but real transformation happens when we step back, take responsibility, and see the bigger picture.

In life, we get caught up in proving our point, winning arguments, or justifying our emotions. But the real path isn't about proving anything—it's about self-awareness. It's about recognizing the patterns we've created and how those patterns shape our experiences. As we mature, we realize it's not about placing blame or pointing fingers. It's about acknowledging our role in shaping our reality and finding the strength to change what no longer serves us.

The hardest truth to accept is that much of our suffering is self-inflicted. We hold on to grudges, fears, and past pain, which only keep us stuck. But when we take full responsibility for our energy and actions, we begin to break the cycles that limit us. Awareness is the first step to healing—it's the key to creating a life that is peaceful, fulfilling, and aligned with our deepest desires.

To move forward, we must stop fighting the past. We must stop blaming the world for our struggles and, instead, turn inward. The truth is that we are the architects of our experiences. Once we accept that, we can begin attracting a life filled with love, peace, and understanding.

The more I learned about myself, the more I realized that overcoming life's tests wasn't about simply pushing through—it was about true self-awareness. I could no longer ignore the lesson that real healing happens when I recognized that the answers I sought were already within me. It's not about seeking validation or measuring one's worth through others' approval. It's about knowing our power lies in how we see ourselves.

The most conflicting realization was accepting that I was responsible for my suffering. At first, I resisted it. I believed my circumstances were beyond my control—that my battles were caused by what others had done to me or by life's unfairness. But the truth was, I had played a role in these challenges, even if unknowingly. I had carried my past into my future, allowing fear to shape my reality.

We often don't realize the damage we cause by allowing ourselves to dwell in negativity. It's not just about the words we speak but the energy we put into the world. The fears we hold onto and the doubts we entertain have a way of shaping our reality. Fear, self-doubt, and self-sabotage kept me stuck for years. But once I acknowledged these patterns, I understood that I had the power to change my life. The key was shifting my mindset—choosing to see possibilities instead of limitations.

I learned to listen to my inner voice. My strength wasn't found in external validation but in stillness, in moments when I truly listened to what my heart and soul were telling me. The guidance had always been there, but I was too distracted by mental noise and outside opinions to hear it. As I began trusting myself, I let go of the belief that I needed approval from others to feel worthy of love and acceptance.

This journey wasn't easy. Some days, it felt like I was making no progress at all. The dread of failure and not being good enough would resurface. But each setback taught me something new, and every lesson made me stronger. I realized that failure wasn't something to fear—it was part of growth. The only real failure is never trying, never facing what scares us the most.

One of my biggest breakthroughs came when I learned to forgive—not just others but myself. Holding onto anger and resentment only tied me to the past. I had to release the guilt of my mistakes and the shame of my perceived failures. In forgiving myself, I finally felt free to move forward. This wasn't just a mental process—it was spiritual. It allowed me to reconnect with who I truly am—a soul on a path of growth and self-discovery.

The path of healing isn't without challenges, but it is one of the most rewarding journeys you can take. When you release fear, stop allowing the past to dictate your future, and begin to understand the strength of your soul, you unlock a power within you that can move mountains. And with that power, there are no limits to what you can achieve.

Healing isn't linear. It doesn't happen overnight, and it's not a destination. It's a lifelong journey. Some days, I still feel the weight of my past, but I now recognize it for what it is—a chapter in my story, not my identity. I am not defined by my past but by how I choose to rise from it.

Through this understanding, I developed a deeper love for myself. The more I embraced my flaws and vulnerabilities, the more room I created for growth and healing. I stopped fighting against myself and started working with myself. I realized that my life, with all its ups and downs, was mine to shape. I no longer felt like a victim of circumstance but the creator of my reality.

Writing this book is my way of letting go and healing. To those who doubted or hurt me—to the bullies, the teachers, and anyone who ever said I wouldn't succeed—thank you. You gave me the greatest realization: failure does not exist. Fear does not exist. There are only obstacles, and they will no longer stand in my way.

CHAPTER 9

THE WORTH OF A DOLLAR

Money is often misunderstood. It is not the root of all evil; money is simply energy. What people choose to do with it determines whether its impact is positive or negative. Evil is not inherent in money—it is a reflection of thoughts, emotions, and intentions.

When we allow ourselves to fear not being able to pay our bills or meet our material needs, we block the flow of abundance. The universe provides endlessly, and when we trust in that, the resources we need will appear. But it requires faith—faith that we are worthy of receiving and that everything we need will come to us at the right time. This is a lesson in trust. When you work in an environment driven solely by money, you begin to see the distortion of human nature. Money itself is just energy, but when people pursue it for the wrong reasons—when they are willing to sacrifice their integrity, their peace, and their values to obtain it—that's when things spiral downward. I worked in industries where profit was the only priority, and the negativity was suffocating. The toxic language, the constant pressure, and the lack of respect for human life drained me. The longer I stayed in that environment, the more it consumed me.

But here's the truth: You don't have to accept that. You don't have to let the negativity of the world swallow you whole. You have the power to shift your energy to uplift yourself and those around you.

You can step away from the noise, the pressure, and the toxicity. You can rise above it.

Consider this: Perhaps someone in a past life, or even in this one, has experienced deep poverty. They may have been homeless, struggling to survive, or constantly worrying about their next meal. In response, they develop an intense desire for money, believing it to be the key to safety and security. They crave it, obsess over it, and allow it to dominate their thoughts. In this pursuit, they may begin lashing out at others, treating people with disrespect, and repeating destructive behaviours learned over time. This cycle continues until someone makes the conscious decision to break free from it.

Too often, we remain in situations—whether a job, a relationship, or a routine—out of fear. Fear of the unknown, fear of financial instability, fear of being alone. These fears keep us trapped in cycles where we are not truly living, only existing. Fear convinces us to stay in jobs that do not align with our values, where we are disrespected and forced to compromise our morals just to earn a paycheck. This endless chase for financial security—at the cost of our happiness—can last for years, leaving us emotionally, physically, and spiritually depleted. We feel stuck, questioning whether it is all worth it.

We are often conditioned to believe in certain ideas, and when these beliefs are passed down through generations, they take root in us, shaping our behaviours and thought patterns. It is easy to fall into these cycles and allow them to dictate our lives. But the gift of being human is that we have the power to choose a different path. This is why I left the industry I was in. The long hours, the lack of appreciation, the toxic environment—it was depleting my soul. But the hardest part of that journey wasn't just leaving; it was realizing that I had to walk away, not just for my well-being, but for something greater—something that would allow me to serve humanity in a more meaningful way.

The truth is money is not everything. Yes, it is necessary for survival, and when used wisely, it can bring about great things. But money is not the foundation of happiness. When you are guided by love, compassion, and purpose, money becomes a tool—a means to an end, not the end itself. My motivation is not wealth; it is service. I want to grow my business, expand my podcast, and build meaningful relationships with people. These are the things that fuel me—not the pursuit of money itself. We need to focus on creating energy rooted in love, positivity, and growth rather than allowing fear to control our decisions.

The key to a fulfilling life isn't found in chasing money or external validation. It lies in trusting yourself, believing in your worth, and having the courage to change what no longer serves you. When you do that, you will begin to see the abundance that has been waiting for you all along.

CHAPTER 10
RELATIONSHIPS

Now, let's talk about relationships. Many of us experience heartbreak, and while it is painful, we must understand that these experiences are guiding us toward something better—something more meaningful. Each failed relationship carries a lesson—sometimes many—that, when embraced, helps us grow. They teach us emotional maturity, self-worth, and the true value of love.

Have you ever been broken up with for being too nice? It's a confusing thing to hear because, in theory, kindness should be a positive trait. But often, when we give too much of ourselves without taking the time to understand our own needs or establish healthy boundaries, it creates an imbalance. Oversharing can lead to feelings of resentment, not just within ourselves but in our partners as well. So, why does this happen? Why can excessive kindness sometimes push people away?

Being too nice often comes from a place of deep sincerity—a genuine desire to make the other person happy. You want to impress them, make them feel valued, and express the love you carry inside. But if you're not careful, you can lose yourself in the process. You become so focused on meeting their needs that you forget to honour your own. This creates an unhealthy dynamic where your partner may feel overwhelmed by your constant giving, and you may end up feeling unappreciated, emotionally drained, or even neglected.

The first relationship is always an eye-opening experience. For me, it was filled with lessons and self-discovery, particularly in understanding myself and my boundaries. One of the most significant challenges I faced was being too nice. I went out of my way to please my partner, to impress them, to express love and affection in abundance. Yet, somehow, this kindness was misinterpreted. My relationship ended because my partner felt overwhelmed, as if they were being smothered. It was a painful realization, but one I had to confront: my need to be liked, to be loved, led me to overextend myself in ways that ultimately harmed the relationship.

In my own experience, my relationships often felt like uphill battles—challenges I unknowingly created because of my fears and insecurities. I struggled with low self-esteem. I didn't believe I was attractive enough, smart enough, or worthy of the kind of love I deeply desired. This lack of self-belief had a profound impact on my relationships. I'd get upset easily, misinterpret situations, and sabotage my happiness out of fear—fear of not being enough, fear of being unlovable.

That fear was the root of many of my emotional reactions. I remember staying in a relationship, not out of love but out of fear—fear that my partner would leave me for someone else. The trauma of past relationships still haunted me, influencing my actions. I wasn't fully present in the relationship because I was too busy anticipating the worst. I avoided deep emotional investment, convinced that rejection, abandonment, or hurt were inevitable. Instead of nurturing a healthy connection, I sought superficial relationships, bouncing from one person to another, trying to fill the void left by past pain.

Fear plays a significant role in relationships too. Many people remain in relationships because they fear being alone. They convince themselves that they are in love, but deep down, they may simply fear the emptiness of being single. They stay in unfulfilling relationships for years, hoping things will improve, yet knowing they are not truly happy. The fear of leaving, the fear of being unloved, and the fear of uncertainty prevent them from making necessary changes for their well-being.

For example, when working in a job where everyone is unhappy, and the culture is built on fear—fear of losing the job, fear of financial instability, fear of disappointing others—you are constantly feeding your anxiety. It becomes a toxic cycle. You may have money in your pocket, but emotionally, you are bankrupt. You are not thriving in the ways that matter most—spiritually, mentally, or emotionally.

In these situations, we compromise our happiness and emotional well-being for the sake of comfort and familiarity. But staying in a toxic relationship or a job that drains you only holds you back. When you are in a toxic environment—whether in your personal life or career—it weighs down your energy. You create a cycle of unhappiness, and because of this, you attract more negativity. You remain stuck.

I also struggled with receiving constructive criticism. Whenever a partner offered me advice, I often took it as an insult. Instead of seeing it as a loving attempt to help me grow, I interpreted it as a judgment of my intelligence or worth. This defensiveness stemmed from deep insecurity. The trauma from past relationships had made me overly sensitive, and I reacted by lashing out. I couldn't separate the criticism from my fear that I wasn't good enough.

Bringing past trauma into adulthood doesn't just affect romantic relationships—it influences our connections with family, friends, and colleagues. When fear shapes our perspective, even well-meaning criticism from a loved one can feel like an attack instead of an opportunity for growth. In response, we retreat, put up walls, and shut people out rather than confronting the pain that lingers. This fear isolates us, preventing the meaningful connections we long for.

This is the challenge with trauma—it builds walls that make communication difficult. When wounds from the past remain unhealed, these barriers prevent deep connections with others. Open communication becomes nearly impossible, trapping you in a cycle of misunderstandings and hurt feelings. Instead of creating love and respect, you go through the motions of being in a relationship without fully engaging with your partner.

Communication is one of the most challenging aspects of any relationship, especially when emotional baggage weighs you down. Without open and honest communication, nothing can be resolved. It's easy to settle into complacency—to remain in a relationship out of fear of being alone, even if it no longer brings happiness. Fear keeps you trapped in cycles of unhealthy behaviour, and as a result, your relationships suffer.

I realized that for any relationship to thrive, I first had to do the inner work. I needed to confront my fears, heal old wounds, and rebuild my self-worth. Until I worked on myself, I couldn't expect a relationship to succeed. Every failed relationship revealed that I wasn't ready—either I was attracting dynamics that didn't align with what I truly wanted, or I was still holding on to fears that kept me from fully connecting with my partner.

Relationships follow the same pattern. If you find yourself trapped in an endless cycle of arguments, misunderstandings, and dissatisfaction, it is a reflection of your inner state. You may believe that you have fallen out of love, but often, fear is what keeps you tethered to that person. You stay because you are afraid of being alone, afraid of not finding someone else, afraid of change. But in the end, it is this very fear that keeps the problems alive.

If you find yourself stuck in the same painful cycles, ask yourself: What am I afraid of? What unresolved trauma is still influencing my present relationships? Only by confronting these questions and engaging in deep self-reflection can you break free from the patterns that hold you back. Healing isn't easy, but it's the path to the love and connection you truly deserve.

Here's the truth: until you heal from past wounds, your relationships will reflect that inner chaos. If fear, insecurity, or unresolved hurt drive your actions, those emotions will shape your relationship patterns. You will continue attracting partners or situations that reinforce the same emotional struggles. But when you commit to healing, everything shifts. Your energy changes, and with that shift, the right relationships begin to enter your life—connections built on mutual love, respect, and emotional support.

So, the real question is: How long will you stay in a relationship, job, or situation that no longer serves you? How long will you ignore the signs and deny your unhappiness? Only you have the power to break free. And when you do, you will come to realize that you were never truly stuck. You can change your circumstances at any time.

Remember, the most important relationship you will ever have is the one you have with yourself. Only when you truly love and accept yourself can you build healthy, meaningful relationships with others. If you've experienced past pain, don't let it define you—let it be a lesson, not a burden. You can change, grow, and attract the love you deserve. But that journey starts with healing from the past and embracing who you are right now.

Chapter 11:
Trust Your Body, It Knows You Best

We often get so caught up in our self-centred tendencies and stubbornness that we fail to recognize the damage we cause—not only to ourselves but also to those around us. The hardest truth to accept is that many of our struggles are of our own making, and coming to terms with that can be painful. We resist taking responsibility for the things that aren't going right in our lives. It's easier to blame external circumstances than to acknowledge that we might be the ones standing in our own way.

One of the main reasons we don't reach our goals is that we choose to diminish ourselves. We absorb too much of what others think and, in doing so, silence our inner voice. We forget that our inner guidance is the most valuable—it is the voice that truly understands our needs and identity. Instead of living with intention, we merely go through the motions, existing rather than thriving. We get pulled into cycles of negativity without even realizing that the source of that negativity is often within us.

This was a powerful realization I had during my spiritual journey. I once believed I was healed, but as I explored deeper, I understood that healing isn't a destination—it's a continuous process. It never truly ends. The moment we believe we are fully healed is often when we uncover new layers of ourselves that still need attention. An effective tool

I've found in managing this ongoing growth is self-reflection—whether through journaling or confiding in someone I trust. By expressing my emotions, I realize I freed myself from the burdens I would otherwise carry alone.

Saying this, we must also be mindful of how we react to the energy and opinions of others. When someone offers negativity or criticism, we should ask ourselves why it affects us so deeply. More often than not, the reason is that we are still holding onto unresolved pain. Our bodies communicate with us when we are out of balance, and it's our responsibility to listen. Ignoring these subtle signals only allows discomfort to grow, eventually manifesting in ways we can no longer ignore.

Nothing in life happens by accident. Every experience carries meaning, no matter how insignificant we may believe it to be at the time. When we disregard the messages our bodies send, discomfort intensifies as a drastic way to demand our attention. Our goal should be to build a deeper connection with ourselves, to understand our bodies, and to treat them with care and respect. When we practice self-compassion, our bodies respond with renewed strength and vitality. However, the moment we begin to neglect or criticize ourselves, we invite distress—often in the form of illness, fatigue, or discomfort.

I started noticing how my body reacted when I ignored the signs. At first, I brushed it off, assuming it was just a rough day or random stress. But over time, I realized the discomfort wasn't random—it was my body pleading for attention. The stiffness in my neck, the persistent headaches, the tightness in my chest—these weren't just passing inconveniences. They were signals urging me to pause, take a breath, and address the unresolved emotions I had been neglecting.

What matters most is silencing the voices and thoughts that pull you away from healing. Don't allow external influences to control how you feel. Your emotions belong to you alone, and they are entirely valid. Healing is deeply personal, but it becomes even more powerful when you learn to trust your body and your inner guidance. By strengthening this connection, you align more closely with your true self, and that is where real transformation begins.

So, what daily steps can we take to create a stronger connection with our bodies? It all begins with awareness. Our thoughts have the power to support or disrupt our well-being. If we're feeling overwhelmed or unsteady, we must pause and reflect. Ask yourself:

"Why am I feeling this way? What has triggered this imbalance? How can I work with myself to regain stability and move forward with clarity?"

You might find this confusing at first, and that's perfectly okay. When I first started learning these principles, I felt the same way too. To be honest, I sort of felt crazy. But over time, you'll begin to trust yourself and the wisdom within you. The people around you don't determine how your day unfolds—you do. If you're not happy with who you are, take a moment to ask yourself why. Your body, mind, and inner self already hold the answers. It's natural to feel resistance or uncertainty in the beginning, but don't let that discourage you. Give it time.

Chapter 12: Quiet the Mind

As we continue exploring the theme of healing, it becomes clear that our bodies are powerful messengers. When we feel unsettled, anxious, or overwhelmed, it's not just our minds reacting—our bodies are speaking to us. Every suppressed emotion and every ignored thought will eventually manifest in our physical state. It's essential to pay attention and understand what our bodies are trying to communicate.

Connecting with Your Body

A valuable observation I am continuously learning is how to build a deeper, more meaningful connection with my body. This correlation is essential for healing. It's not just about addressing physical symptoms—it's about identifying the origin of why you're feeling this way.

When we start paying closer attention to how we feel physically, we gain clearer insight into what's happening emotionally and mentally. These physical cues serve as reminders to look within and ask ourselves the hard questions:

Why am I feeling tense today? Why am I holding on to this anger or frustration? What unresolved emotions am I carrying?

Example: *"I used to feel frustrated every time I had a headache, believing it was just something I had to push through. But now, I pause. I take a deep breath. I ask myself, 'What's happening in my life that's contributing to this tension?' And* *in that moment of awareness, I begin to see where I need to shift my emotional focus."*

The Impact of Negative Energy

The concept of energy is powerful, yet we often overlook how deeply our emotions are connected to it. Every emotion—whether uplifting or draining—carries energy. Negative emotions such as fear, anger, and sadness create tension within us. They can deplete us physically and mentally, leaving us feeling stuck in a cycle of negativity.

When we allow negative energy to remain in our bodies and minds for too long, it becomes toxic. It slows us down, clouds our judgment, and keeps us from making progress in our lives. The longer we hold onto it, the harder it becomes to let go. That's why it's essential to check in with ourselves regularly and release any negative energy before it builds up and takes a greater toll.

Example: *"When we hold onto anger or resentment, we carry a burden that weighs us down. Imagine walking with a backpack filled with heavy stones. The longer you carry it, the more exhausting it becomes. Eventually, the strain becomes too much, and you start to break down. Letting go of negative energy is like setting that heavy backpack down—it allows you to move forward with greater ease and clarity."*

The Power of Self-Talk

During this journey, I noted the power of self-talk is frequently underestimated. The way we speak to ourselves shapes not only how we see the world but also how we see ourselves. When we choose words filled with kindness, compassion, and understanding, we create a strong foundation for healing. However, when we speak to ourselves harshly or critically, we reinforce negative beliefs and drain our energy.

Changing the way we talk to ourselves is laborious, but it is one of the most transformative shifts we can make. Instead of saying, "I can't do this," try saying, "I'm learning how to do this." Instead of thinking, "I'm not good enough," replace it with, "I am enough, and I'm doing my best." These small yet intentional changes in self-talk can create a ripple effect of positivity.

Example: *"There was a time when I would criticize myself harshly every time I made a mistake. I'd say, 'You're so stupid,' or 'You'll never get this right.' But over time, I learned to replace those hurtful words with more encouraging ones. Now, when I stumble, I remind myself, 'It's okay. I'm learning, and I'm going to improve.'"*

Listening to Your Inner Voice

Your inner voice is one of the most powerful guides on your journey of healing and personal growth. It's the voice that speaks the truth when you need it most, even when your mind is clouded by doubt or fear. Learning to trust this voice is essential to moving forward.

However, tuning into your inner voice isn't always easy. We often become so consumed by the noise of daily life that we struggle to distinguish it from the distractions around us. But when you quiet your mind and create space for stillness, that voice becomes clearer. Silence the static.

Example: *"At first, I couldn't hear my inner voice. It was buried beneath fear and self-doubt. But as I practiced meditation and gave myself quiet moments to reflect, that voice grew louder. It was the voice of love, truth, and guidance, reminding me, 'You are enough,' and 'You are worthy of love and success.'"*

Creating Healthy Boundaries

One of the most effective ways to protect our energy and emotions is by setting healthy boundaries. Boundaries help us safeguard our personal space and prevent negativity from overwhelming us. Whether it's limiting time spent with draining individuals, saying no to situations that deplete us, or carving out moments for self-care, boundaries are essential for maintaining mental, emotional, and physical well-being.

Setting boundaries is in no form an act of selfishness—it's an act of self-respect and self-care. It allows you to prioritize your well-being, which in turn enables you to be more present and giving toward others. This agreement with self is non-negotiable.

Example: *"For years, I struggled with saying no. I worried that setting boundaries would make me seem selfish or unkind. But when I began to say no to things that left me emotionally exhausted, I noticed a shift. I felt more at peace and more capable of giving to others from a place of wholeness."*

Chapter 13:
The Power of Integration and Moving Forward

After an awakening, it's easy to believe the journey is complete—we've arrived at some final destination of understanding. But awakening is just the beginning. It marks the first step on a much longer path. This not only requires continuous growth, self-exploration, and the integration of lessons we've uncovered along the way.

When I first experienced my awakening, everything felt fresh, new, and full of possibility. The world seemed clearer, and I had a deep sense of certainty that I was on the right path. But soon, I realized that awakening doesn't mean life suddenly becomes effortless. It's not about avoiding challenges—it's about learning to move through them with greater awareness, wisdom, and grace.

The next step after awakening is integration. This is where we take the insights and knowledge we've gained and apply them to our daily lives. It's about aligning our thoughts, actions, and behaviours with the deeper truths we've uncovered within ourselves.

But integration isn't always easy. It can be messy, uncomfortable, and even painful at times. The reality is that when your perspective shifts, everything in your life begins to reflect that change—your relationships, your career, your health, and your goals. Sometimes, this means letting go of old patterns, beliefs, or relationships that no longer align with who you are becoming. Growth requires releasing what no longer serves you.

Letting go of the past isn't about rejecting it or labelling it as wrong. It's about recognizing that every experience played a role in shaping the person you are today. As you continue forward, you'll begin to see that every moment—every challenge, heartbreak, and triumph—has been preparing you for this phase of your life.

The process of integration is much like assembling a puzzle—there are scattered pieces, and your task is to bring them together. But it's not about forcing the pieces to fit. It's about allowing everything to align naturally. It requires patience, self-compassion, and the understanding that you don't need to have all the answers right away.

Integration is also about trusting the timing of your life. It's easy to feel frustrated when things don't unfold as quickly as you'd like, but there's purpose in every pause. Every delay is an opportunity to reflect, recalibrate, and ensure that your next step aligns with your highest good.

There will be moments when you feel lost or uncertain—when the path ahead isn't as clear as you'd hoped. These moments are not signs of failure but of transformation. They are invitations to surrender, to release the need for control, and to trust that the universe, your higher self, and your intuition are leading you exactly where you need to be.

As I moved forward after my awakening, I realized I couldn't continue living as I had before. I couldn't ignore the truth that had been revealed to me. At the same time, I had to find balance—a way to remain fully engaged with the world around me while staying true to my new understanding of myself and life.

The world often pulls us in different directions, pressuring us to conform to societal expectations and chase external success. But what happens when we choose to step away from that script and instead live in alignment with our inner truth? Moving forward means staying true to yourself, even if it requires stepping off the familiar path. It's not about striving for perfection—it's about embracing authenticity.

It's about honouring your pace, trusting your journey, and resisting the urge to compare it to anyone else's.

Moving forward doesn't require having all the answers. It means remaining open to new experiences and trusting that each step is guiding you toward a deeper understanding or a necessary lesson. Growth isn't a race—it's a process that unfolds in its own time.

You are exactly where you need to be.

The next phase of your life isn't about reaching a final destination—it's about living each day with awareness, purpose, and intention. It's about trusting life's unfolding, even when the path ahead is unclear.

In this chapter, you'll learn to lean into the discomfort of transformation and embrace the unknown with confidence. As you integrate the wisdom gained from your awakening, you'll come to realize that you are capable of handling whatever comes your way. You're no longer the person you once were—you've grown, evolved, and stepped into a deeper understanding of yourself.

There will be moments when it feels like you're taking two steps forward and one step back. That's okay. Growth isn't linear—it's a cycle. You'll revisit old patterns, but each time with greater awareness and stronger tools to face them. Every time you come full circle, you'll find yourself on higher ground, better equipped to move through life's challenges with resilience and grace.

This period of integration is also about forgiveness—both for yourself and others. Forgive yourself for the mistakes you made when you didn't know better. Forgive yourself for the times you acted out of fear instead of wisdom. And just as importantly, forgive others, because holding onto resentment only keeps you tethered to the past.

What I've learned is that moving forward doesn't mean having all the answers. It means being open to new experiences and trusting that each step you take is leading you to your next lesson or revelation. It's about allowing yourself to evolve at your own pace—without comparison, without pressure—embracing your unique journey.

Life will continue to test you. New challenges will emerge, and old fears, doubts, and insecurities may resurface. But with each test, you will grow stronger, wiser, and more resilient. Your journey is far from over—it's just beginning.

It's not about how quickly you reach your goals. It's about showing up for yourself every day with courage and faith, knowing that each step is part of a larger, more meaningful journey.

Chapter 14: Embracing Change and Transformation

Introduction: The Call to Change

Change is inevitable, yet it often stirs fear and resistance. Many people hesitate to embrace it—even when it holds the potential for positive transformation—because they fear the unknown. But change is not an obstacle; it is a doorway to growth.

I once resisted change myself.

"For years, I avoided change. Every time something unfamiliar presented itself, I turned away, convincing myself I wasn't ready or that it was too uncertain. But deep down, I knew that staying in my comfort zone meant staying in the same place forever—never moving forward, never evolving. It wasn't until I finally accepted change, with all the discomfort that came with it, that I truly began to grow."

Before we begin, take a moment. Find a quiet space. Pour your favourite hot beverage. Grab a notebook and pen. This is where your transformation begins. Let's go.

Section 1: The Fear of Change

Why do we fear change, even when it leads to something better? Fear of the unknown, failure, and loss of control are deeply rooted psychological patterns. We often cling to familiar habits, even when they no longer serve us, simply because they feel safe.

Fear can manifest subtly: procrastination, self-sabotage, or indecision. Sometimes we don't even realize we're resisting change. But the truth is, fear is not an enemy. It is a natural response to uncertainty—and it can be overcome.

"The most challenging part of change is the fear it brings. We fear failure, looking foolish, and the discomfort of stepping out of the familiar. But this fear isn't just an obstacle—it's an opportunity to prove to ourselves that we are capable of far more than we give ourselves credit for."

Section 2: The Power of Letting Go

Letting go is a vital part of transformation. Whether it's old habits, unhealthy relationships, or outdated beliefs, clinging to the past keeps us stuck. Releasing those weights makes space for something new.

Letting go doesn't mean forgetting. It means honoring the past, learning from it, and moving forward with wisdom. The emotional process can be intense, but it brings freedom and clarity.

"Letting go is never easy. It's like shedding a layer of yourself that you've worn for years, even when it no longer fits. But holding onto old wounds, grudges, and limiting beliefs only keeps us trapped in a past that no longer serves us. Letting go is not about forgetting; it's about creating space for something better."

Section 3: The Discomfort of Transformation

Transformation is rarely comfortable. Like a caterpillar in its cocoon, we must struggle to break through our own barriers to emerge renewed.

Discomfort is often mistaken for danger. But in truth, it is evidence of growth. The pain of shedding old identities is what allows us to expand into our highest potential.

"Transformation is uncomfortable, and that's okay. Just as a caterpillar struggles to break free from its cocoon, we, too, must push past our old selves. It can feel

uncertain and even painful, but it is a necessary part of growth. Instead of resisting discomfort, welcome it—it is proof that you are evolving."

Section 4: Shifting Your Mindset

Your mindset is the foundation of your transformation. A fixed mindset says, "This is who I am." A growth mindset whispers, "This is who I can become."

By choosing to pivot your thinking, you unlock the door to healing, expansion, and success. Internal shifts create external change.

"A fixed mindset convinces you that change is impossible—that this is just the way things are. But a growth mindset opens the door to new possibilities. It reminds you that no matter where you are right now, you can change and improve. The key is to be patient and trust that every step you take is guiding you toward a stronger, more capable version of yourself."

Section 5: Taking Action

Transformation doesn't happen by thought alone—it requires action. Consistent, intentional steps are what move you from wishing to becoming.

Here are five foundational actions to support your transformation:

1. Learn to be comfortable in your own company.
2. Deepen your self-understanding.
3. Identify your emotional triggers and where they come from.
4. Learn to communicate authentically with others.
5. Show up as the empowered version of yourself—the one who is ready, willing, and worthy.

Section 6: Embracing the New You

Becoming someone, new means creating non-negotiable goals and holding yourself accountable to the future you. The hardest part? The old you will try to pull you back.

But every moment you choose alignment over avoidance, healing over hiding, and love over fear, you grow.

As you step into change, you'll realize that you are no longer the person you once were. You are evolving, growing, and becoming more aligned with your true self. Welcome this new version of yourself—it's a powerful reflection of the effort and dedication you've poured into your transformation."

Conclusion: The Journey of Transformation

Transformation is not a single event. It is a lifelong unfolding.

You will face resistance. You will be tested. But within you is the strength to move forward—again and again.

"Transformation is a journey, not a destination. It's about embracing every moment, every challenge, and every step forward. You have the power to achieve whatever you commit to. Don't fear change—welcome it, because through change, you will uncover your true strength."

You are becoming. Keep going.

Chapter 15:
The Process of Change and Failure

Change is one of the few constants in life, yet it's often met with resistance. Whether it's changing jobs, relationships, locations, or even a way of life, transitions are almost always accompanied by fear. The fear of change—especially the fear of failure—holds many people back from stepping into new possibilities. But what if those fears are actually the doorway to a more fulfilling life?

Necessary Changes Within Life

Life is built on patterns, routines, and familiar comforts. When things feel predictable, they offer a sense of security. Even when a part of you recognizes that you've outgrown your current path, the thought of change can feel overwhelming. The fear of change often stems from a deep psychological attachment—to your identity, the life you've built, or the way others perceive you.

A shift—whether in direction, mindset, or lifestyle—can stir up unsettling questions: "Who am I if I let go of the old me?" or "What if I don't succeed in this new life?"

However, true growth comes from embracing life's transitions. When we allow ourselves to break free from old patterns, we uncover strengths and aspects of ourselves we never knew existed. Change isn't about losing who you are—it's about stepping into who you're meant to become. It's about giving yourself permission to release what no longer serves you and opening the door to new opportunities for growth, fulfillment, and joy.

Evolving in Relationships

Relationships are one of the most profound areas where the fear of change often arises. Whether it's letting go of old friendships, transitioning out of a romantic partnership, or redefining family dynamics, these shifts can feel like a loss. As social beings, we find comfort in the bonds we create. They provide a sense of belonging and security, and the thought of losing them can feel overwhelming.

But as we grow, so do our relationships. What once served us in one season of life may no longer align with who we are becoming. The fear of losing relationships can cause us to cling to connections that may actually be holding us back. Embracing the natural evolution of relationships—whether by adjusting the dynamics of an existing one or making space for healthier connections—can lead to unexpected depth and fulfillment.

Change in relationships doesn't always mean an ending; sometimes, it marks a transformation into something more genuine and aligned with who you are now.

Pursuing Your True Career

The fear of changing jobs is often rooted in the need for stability. Work provides financial security, identity, and structure. For many, the thought of leaving a steady job to pursue a new career—or even riskier, to follow a passion—can feel overwhelming. What if it doesn't work out? What if I fail? These fears keep many people from pursuing the work that truly excites them.

However, prioritizing passion and fulfillment in your work can lead to a more meaningful and satisfying life. Staying in a job that no longer inspires you—simply out of fear of failure—keeps you stagnant. The truth is that remaining in a role that no longer aligns with you often leads to burnout and dissatisfaction. Change creates space for new opportunities, fresh challenges, and a renewed sense of purpose. Overcoming the fear of changing jobs begins with shifting your mindset—

not as a reckless leap into uncertainty, but as a step toward discovering a path that truly resonates with you.

The Fear of Changing Locations

The fear of changing locations—whether that means moving to a new city, country, or even a different neighbourhood—can bring a deep sense of uncertainty. We thrive on familiarity, and uprooting ourselves from the place we've called home can feel like stepping away from the comfort of our established routines, communities, and memories. The fear of change can hold us back from embracing life in a new setting— one that may offer unexpected opportunities for growth and renewal.

While leaving behind the familiar can feel overwhelming, relocating has the potential to shift perspectives and create new possibilities. A new environment may push you beyond your comfort zone, but it also introduces you to fresh experiences, connections, and personal growth. Often, the fear of changing locations disguises the opportunity for a deeper connection to yourself and the world around you. Moving doesn't have to be permanent to be transformative—it's about giving yourself the freedom to step into a new space where you can evolve, free from old limitations.

Overcoming the Fear of Change and Failure

Ultimately, all these fears stem from the same place: a desire for security. We fear what we don't understand, and we fear failure because it threatens our sense of stability. But what if failure isn't a setback? What if it's simply a step toward growth, learning, and self-discovery?

To overcome the fear of change and failure, shifting your mindset is essential. Instead of viewing change as something to fear, embrace it as an opportunity for expansion. Instead of seeing failure as defeat, recognize it as a necessary part of progress—often the very thing that leads to long-term success. When you allow yourself to step into the discomfort of new experiences, you open yourself to unexpected possibilities, deeper connections, and greater personal fulfillment.

Remember, change is inevitable—it's how we respond to it that shapes our growth. The fear you feel in moments of transition isn't a sign to retreat; it's a signal that you're on the edge of something new, something transformative. Trust yourself, trust the process, and take that first step. You already have everything you need to move through the unknown and build the life, relationships, and career you desire.

Chapter 16:
Conquering Failure in Life

The Weight of Expectations

The fear of failure often begins with the burden of expectations—both external and internal. From an early age, we are conditioned to succeed: we are taught to aim for high grades, climb the social ladder, build careers, and maintain stable relationships. Society, family, and even peers place immense pressure on us to "get it right" and avoid mistakes.

But carrying the weight of these expectations can leave us feeling trapped. The fear of failure becomes less about actual consequences and more about the belief that failing equates to being unworthy or incapable. Life doesn't follow a singular path, yet failure often feels like the end of one. In reality, failure is simply part of the process. Whether it's struggling on an exam, losing a job, or experiencing the breakdown of a relationship, every setback carries an opportunity for growth.

The Pressure of Judgment

Much of our fear of failure stems from the fear of judgment. The worry about how others perceive us—whether they see us as weak, unworthy, or incapable—can keep us from taking action. We often internalize the opinions of others, allowing their perceptions to shape our self-worth as if they define our truth. This fear can leave us feeling stuck, making it seem safer to do nothing at all than to risk failing in front of others.

But the fear of judgment is often an illusion. The truth is, most people are too caught up in their own lives to scrutinize ours as harshly as we imagine. And those who do judge are often projecting their own insecurities. The key is to shift your focus inward—on your growth, your learning, and the understanding that every setback is a stepping stone toward success.

The Desire for Perfection

Perfectionism often fuels the fear of failure. Many people hesitate to take action because they believe that anything less than flawless execution equates to failure. However, this mindset creates a barrier. Perfection is an illusion—an unattainable goal that keeps us stuck. The relentless pursuit of flawlessness can prevent progress, making us afraid to take risks or try something new.

Accepting imperfection is essential. Failure becomes less intimidating when we realize that success isn't about perfection but about growth. Real learning comes from experience, especially in moments that feel messy or uncertain. Every mistake or misstep is an opportunity to gain insight and move closer to our goals.

Reframing Failure as Growth

Reframing failure is essential to overcoming the fear of it. Instead of viewing failure as a measure of our worth, we can recognize it as a crucial step toward success. Some of the most accomplished individuals in history have faced repeated setbacks before achieving their goals. Thomas Edison made thousands of attempts before perfecting the light bulb, and J.K. Rowling endured countless rejections before Harry Potter was published.

Failure does not define your potential—it provides an opportunity to refine your approach, reassess your strategies, and grow stronger. It is through failure that we build resilience, creativity, and the courage to keep moving forward.

Living Beyond Possibilities

Living a fulfilling life requires stepping beyond our comfort zones and embracing the uncertainty that comes with not always succeeding. It means recognizing that failure is inevitable—not as something to fear but as an essential part of a rich and meaningful life.

To overcome the fear of failure, we must first accept ourselves fully, including our imperfections. We need to let go of the need for external validation and learn to trust ourselves—our intuition, our passions, and our ability to rise from failure stronger than before.

Acting Despite the Fear

Action is the antidote to fear. Every time you take a step forward despite the fear of failure, you prove to yourself that you are capable. It's about taking small, consistent steps toward your dreams, knowing that every effort—no matter how minor—moves you forward. And even when you stumble or fall short, what matters most is that you keep going. Every setback carries a lesson that strengthens you.

The fear of failure often stems from the belief that we are not good enough or unworthy of success. But your worth is not measured by your failures—it is measured by your willingness to try, to grow, and to persevere.

Chapter 17:
The Fear of Death and Embracing the Unknown

The fear of death is one of the most universal and deeply ingrained fears in the human experience. It's not just about the physical act of dying but about the vast unknown that follows. This fear influences our decisions, shapes our actions, and even affects our relationships. It lingers in the background of daily life, often unspoken yet ever-present. We hesitate to discuss it openly, and we structure our lives in ways that keep it at a distance. At its core, the fear of death is a fear of the unknown. What happens when we take our final breath? Will it hurt? Will we be remembered? These unanswered questions weigh on many, yet they are often pushed aside, too uncomfortable to confront.

As a society, we have developed countless ways to avoid facing death directly. It remains a taboo subject—an uncomfortable truth we try to ignore, avoiding the difficult conversations and emotions it stirs. Instead of accepting death as a natural part of life, we build elaborate rituals around it—funerals, wakes, and memorials—all designed to soften its impact. We tell ourselves that death is "far away," as if ignoring it will somehow delay or prevent it. But avoidance only strengthens the fear. The longer we refuse to face it, the more power it holds over us. By keeping it in the shadows, we allow it to take a deeper root in our minds.

There is a certain peace that comes with accepting death—not as an end, but as a natural part of existence. Death is simply one chapter in the vast, ongoing story of life. Acknowledging this truth releases its hold on us. It frees us to live more fully, recognizing that every moment is valuable. Life and death are not opposing forces but interconnected aspects of the same reality. Death is the counterpart to birth, the closing of one door as another opens. When we embrace this understanding, we begin to see both as essential to the continuous process of becoming.

The fear of death is, in many ways, an ancient survival mechanism wired into our biology. For our ancestors, this fear was a vital tool for survival. It triggered the fight-or-flight response, sharpening their instincts and compelling them to avoid danger at all costs. This instinct ensured the continuation of the human species. While modern life no longer presents the same immediate threats, our brains remain programmed to fear and resist death.

Culturally, our understanding of death has been shaped by our beliefs and philosophies. Religious and spiritual teachings offer various explanations and reassurances, from the promise of an afterlife to the concept of reincarnation or eternal rest. Yet even these perspectives do not always erase the fear entirely. There is always a lingering uncertainty—what if our beliefs are wrong? What if death is nothing more than an empty void? It is this uncertainty that fuels our fear.

On a psychological level, the fear of death is often linked to deeper fears—the fear of losing control, the fear of leaving loved ones behind, and the fear of not having lived a meaningful life. These fears create a cycle of anxiety and uncertainty surrounding mortality. Yet, within this uncertainty lies the opportunity to embrace life fully. Instead of allowing fear to consume us, we can choose to step into the unknown with openness and courage.

The idea of embracing the unknown may seem overwhelming, but it holds the key to personal growth. The unknown is not just a source of fear—it is also a space for discovery and transformation. While we cannot predict when our final moment will come, accepting uncertainty allows us to live with intention and purpose. This shift in perspective opens the door to deeper experiences, stronger connections, and the freedom to live authentically.

I recall a time in my life when fear held me back—not just the fear of death, but the fear of change. Whether in relationships, career decisions, or personal growth, change often feels like a small death. It forces us to step away from the familiar and embrace the unpredictable. There was a time when this fear of the unknown kept me stuck. I hesitated to take risks or pursue new opportunities because I feared failure or regret. But with time, I realized that facing the unknown was the only way to find peace. Letting go of control and trusting the process brought me a sense of freedom—and, with it, joy. This lesson stays with me: when we release fear and lean into uncertainty, we free ourselves from its grip and step into a life of purpose.

Tools like mindfulness help ground us in the present moment, easing the anxiety of what's to come. Practicing mindfulness does not mean ignoring the future; rather, it teaches us to acknowledge our thoughts without allowing them to control us. By staying rooted in the present, we reduce our tendency to worry about death and instead focus on living in a way that honours the value of each moment.

Spirituality can also offer deep comfort when confronting the fear of death. Whether through faith in a higher power, meditation, or a belief in the interconnectedness of all life, spiritual practices help reframe our understanding of existence. These belief systems provide a sense of meaning, offering solace in the face of the unknown. Even without religious affiliation, recognizing the interconnectedness of all life—the idea that we are part of something greater—can bring a profound sense of peace.

One of the most powerful ways to confront the fear of death is by shifting our mindset. Instead of seeing death as an end, we can begin to view it as a transition. Just as we evolve throughout our lives, so does the universe. Death is not a singular event but a continuation of the natural rhythm of existence—a doorway that leads to the next chapter. When we embrace this perspective, death shifts from being a terrifying prospect to something we can approach with acceptance and grace.

Living fully becomes a natural response to this realization. When we release the grip of fear, we open ourselves to experiencing life in its entirety—the joys, the challenges, and everything in between. We learn to cherish each moment, express love without hesitation, and show up authentically in our relationships. The fear of death, though it may still surface at times, no longer dictates our choices. It fades into the background, no longer holding us captive.

It's important to understand that overcoming the fear of death does not mean eliminating it. Rather, it means transforming our relationship with it. Fear will always exist in some form, but we can learn not to let it control our lives. Journaling can be a powerful tool for processing emotions tied to mortality. Writing down our thoughts brings clarity, helping us work through our fears with greater awareness. Open and honest conversations about death—though uncomfortable at first—can also help demystify it. The more we speak about it, the less intimidating it becomes. Gratitude practices further ground us in the present, allowing us to appreciate life's fleeting beauty without being consumed by its impermanence.

I have been deeply moved by the stories of individuals who have experienced near-death moments and returned with profound insights. Many of them describe a dramatic shift in their outlook—one that is less rooted in fear and more focused on living with intention. They express a deep gratitude for life and a renewed understanding of the connection between all beings. Their experiences teach us that fear when acknowledged and surrendered to, can become a catalyst for growth. In releasing the need to control what is beyond us, we discover peace.

As I reflect on these lessons, I am reminded that life and death are deeply intertwined. Death does not erase the meaning of life—it amplifies it. Each day we live, we contribute to a story that will extend far beyond our time on Earth. Embracing the unknown means accepting that we will never have all the answers. It is about finding peace within the questions and walking forward with courage, faith, and trust that whatever lies ahead is part of a greater, ongoing journey.

What would life look like if we truly embraced the unknown? For me, it has meant approaching each day with a deep sense of gratitude, recognizing that time is both limited and precious. It has meant letting go of the need for control and discovering freedom in surrender. Most importantly, it has meant living with purpose, expressing love freely, and keeping an open heart.

The fear of death is a natural part of the human experience, but it does not have to define us. By facing it, understanding it, and accepting the unknown, we can reshape our perspective. We can choose to live more fully, love more deeply, and walk this path with peace—knowing that the unknown is not something to fear but something to approach with curiosity and trust.

CHAPTER 18:

Fear as the Catalyst for Growth

The Fear I Created

For much of my life, I believed fear was something external—a force beyond my control that dictated my decisions and held me back. I saw fear as a shadow, always looming over me, keeping me from moving forward. But as I examined my thoughts and beliefs more closely, I had a powerful realization: fear wasn't chasing me—I was creating it.

Through the perspective of the law of assumption, I began to see how my thoughts and beliefs shaped my reality. Every time I convinced myself that I wasn't capable, deserving, or worthy, fear would surface, reflecting my own limiting beliefs. I wasn't just encountering fear—I was giving it power. This awareness was both humbling and liberating. If I was the one creating my fears, then I also could release them.

Fear's Hidden Purpose

As I began to confront my fears instead of avoiding them, something unexpected happened. I realized that fear wasn't my enemy. It was my guide.

When I feared failure, it wasn't because I was incapable—it was because I cared deeply about success. When I feared rejection, it wasn't because I didn't belong—it was because connection was essential to me. Fear wasn't meant to paralyze me; it was there to highlight what mattered most.

The truth was that fear was pushing me toward growth. It was urging me to step outside my comfort zone, to move beyond the limits I had imposed on myself. Each time I leaned into my fear, I uncovered strength I didn't know I had and gained clarity about the life I wanted to create.

Fear Led Me to My Purpose

One of my greatest fears was confronting my trauma. For years, I avoided looking inward, afraid of the pain and discomfort it would bring. But fear has a way of persisting—it doesn't disappear until you face it. And when I finally did, I uncovered something transformative: healing.

Acknowledging my fears became the key not only to my personal growth but also to understanding my greater purpose. As I worked through my pain, I felt an undeniable pull to help others do the same. I realized that my fear wasn't just about me—it was guiding me toward something bigger: the desire to support others, especially those who had faced their struggles and traumas.

Rewriting Fear Through the Law of Assumption

The law of assumption became a powerful tool in my life. It showed me that my beliefs shape my reality. When I viewed fear as my enemy, I lived in a cycle of resistance and avoidance. But when I chose to see fear as a catalyst for growth, everything shifted.

I stopped running and started engaging with it by asking:

What are you trying to teach me?

What opportunity lies beyond this discomfort?

How can I use this fear to grow into the person I want to become?

These shifts in perspective transformed fear from an obstacle into a driving force. I no longer saw it as a barrier but as a bridge—one that connected me to my true self and the people I was meant to help.

From Fear to Fulfillment

Today, I see fear differently. It's not something to be conquered or defeated but something to be understood and embraced. Fear has taught me some of life's most valuable lessons:

It revealed what truly matters.

It pushed me to confront my limits and grow beyond them.

It guided me toward my purpose—helping others heal from their fears and traumas.

By working through my fears, I've learned how to help others see their fears not as obstacles but as opportunities. Fear is not a burden—it is a guide, pointing us toward growth, meaning, and fulfillment.

Chapter 19:
Releasing Your Past and Awaken Your Future

During my journey of self-discovery, I came to a difficult realization: working with a psychologist or psychiatrist did not bring me the success I had hoped for. Rather than feeling seen and understood, I felt like just another case file—one more client to be checked off a list. They offered solutions, but it was as if they were speaking a language I couldn't connect with—an approach that failed to recognize me as an individual with my struggles and experiences. It was a humbling moment but also one of clarity. I realized that true healing and personal growth couldn't come solely from external sources; they had to start from within.

The turning point in my growth—especially in becoming a stronger partner in relationships—came when I discovered the power of forgiveness. For me, forgiveness wasn't just about releasing anger toward others; it was about learning to forgive myself. If you can't forgive yourself for past mistakes, you'll always feel weighed down by them. Holding onto resentment, guilt, or regret only keeps you stuck in destructive cycles. And when you carry those emotions, they seep into your relationships. You begin to project them onto the person you're with, unconsciously turning them into reflections of your past fears or even past abusers. Instead of seeing their criticism as constructive, you perceive it as an attack. It becomes a trigger, and before you know it, you're trapped in the same repetitive situations that have defined your past relationships.

The hardest part of this process is letting go. Letting go of past hurts, unrealistic expectations, and the anger that has kept you from growing. But this is where true transformation happens. When you release those burdens, you allow healing to take place. You stop repeating the same relationship mistakes and begin forming deeper, more authentic connections with those around you—especially with the person you choose to share your life with.

As we go through life, we often find ourselves trapped by past trauma, struggling to see the bigger picture and unable to move beyond the discomfort that keeps us stuck. However, I realized that facing this discomfort is necessary for healing. We must reconnect with our inner child—the part of us that still feels vulnerable and hurt—and give it the space to heal. The process of healing isn't linear, and it isn't easy, but it's worth it. You cannot move forward until you confront and release the pain of the past. Only by letting go of anger and resentment can we truly make peace with our history and create space for love, healing, and growth in our present relationships.

It wasn't until I started looking deeper into my reactions—tracing them back to the unresolved pain I had carried for years—that I began to see a way forward. The anger and frustration I felt weren't random; they were tied to wounds I had buried for so long. And the first step toward healing was acknowledging that pain. I had to recognize that my reactions weren't just about the present moment—they were echoes from the past, still alive inside me. Once I understood that, I could finally begin the long and difficult process of working through my trauma.

Looking back at my journey, I now realize how much anger I carried from my childhood—anger that followed me into adulthood and spilled into my relationships. I had no idea how deeply my unresolved pain shaped the way I saw myself and how I interacted with others. I was so consumed by the fear of failure, the fear that I wasn't good enough, that I lost sight of my own worth. That fear kept me from believing in my ability to grow, mature, and evolve into the person I am today. I felt trapped in self-doubt, stuck in an endless cycle of frustration, unable to break free from the beliefs that held me back.

When it came to relationships, fear of communication became one of my greatest obstacles. I struggled because I didn't know how to effectively articulate my emotions. I grew up in an environment where communication was unclear, where emotions were pushed aside, and where sarcasm and harsh words served as a shield. As a result, I developed an overwhelming fear of saying the wrong thing—of making a mistake in conversation, of unintentionally offending someone. It felt like I was constantly walking on eggshells, terrified that the smallest word or action would trigger a negative reaction. That fear built up inside me until it had nowhere else to go. It erupted as anger, rage, and confusion, and I couldn't understand why. It felt like a ticking time bomb inside me, waiting for something—anything—to set it off. And when it did, the aftermath affected not just me but the people I loved.

I've learned that the key to breaking the cycle of destructive relationships isn't about searching for answers outside of yourself—it's about looking inward. Healing starts with you. It begins with forgiving yourself for past mistakes, for the moments you didn't show up as your best self, and for the times you hurt others because you were hurting too. Once you begin to extend that same grace to yourself, it becomes easier to forgive others. That forgiveness is what releases you from the weight of the past, allowing you to step forward with a clear mind and an open heart, ready to build relationships grounded in trust, respect, and love.

One of the hardest lessons I've had to accept is that relationships—especially romantic ones—are not about finding someone to complete you. They're about finding someone who will walk beside you as you heal and grow. But before you can truly connect with someone else, you have to first connect with yourself. That means tending to your wounds, confronting your fears, and making peace with your past. Only then can you become the kind of partner who is emotionally available, and only then can you experience a life-changing, deep and genuine love.

And just remember: growth doesn't happen overnight. It takes time. It takes patience. It requires the courage to look inward—to really see yourself, including the parts you don't want to face. The most difficult part was allowing myself to be vulnerable, to admit that I was afraid, to accept that I didn't have all the answers. But in that vulnerability, I found clarity and strength. And from that clarity, healing finally began.

The real challenge isn't avoiding failure or striving for perfection. The challenge is learning to accept yourself fully, flaws and all, and trusting that, with time and patience, healing is possible. Growth is possible. You can step into the person you were always meant to be. And when you do, you open the door to the kind of healthy, fulfilling relationship you've always longed for. But it all starts with you. It starts with forgiveness. It starts with releasing what no longer serves you. And most importantly, it starts with believing—despite everything you've been through—that you are worthy of love, happiness, and meaningful connection. Once you believe this, the rest of the pieces will naturally fall into place.

A CALL TO ACTION

If you're reading this and feeling trapped by fear, I want to encourage you to shift your perspective. Fear isn't here to destroy you—it's here to guide you. It highlights the areas of your life where you have the greatest opportunity for growth.

Ask yourself: What is your fear trying to teach you? What's waiting for you on the other side? When you embrace fear as a force for transformation, you'll uncover strength, clarity, and purpose like never before.

THE PATH FORWARD - THE JOURNEY OF HEALING

As you continue this healing journey, it's essential to remain present and in tune—with your body, your emotions, and the quiet wisdom of your inner voice.

Healing isn't about perfection or quick fixes; it's about deepening your awareness, nurturing yourself through the highs and lows, and embracing each moment as it comes.

You may stumble. You may struggle. Some days will feel more difficult than others. But each step forward, no matter how small, is progress.

Healing is not a straight path—it twists, turns, and, at times, may feel like you're retracing old ground.

But even in those moments when it seems like nothing is changing, you are growing in ways that may not yet be visible. Trust that the effort you're putting in matters.

Take comfort in knowing that healing has no fixed timeline. You don't have to meet anyone else's expectations—not society's, not even your own past self's.

What matters most is showing up for yourself, consistently and gently, day after day. Honour your rhythm and permit yourself to rest when you need to.

As you continue this path, embrace patience. Remain gentle with yourself as you would a child.

Healing calls for tenderness, especially when old wounds resurface. Meet yourself with kindness, recognizing the strength it takes to confront pain and the courage it takes to seek change.

Celebrate the small victories—the moments when you choose peace over anger, when you sit with discomfort instead of running from it, when you extend forgiveness to yourself instead of criticism.

The only thing that will limit your success is your frame of mind.

You are worthy of all the grace and love this world has to offer.

Don't ever forget it.

-Andrew. Wilson

ABOUT THE AUTHOR

Andrew is a passionate storyteller, healer, and seeker dedicated to helping others unlock their true potential. With years of experience navigating his path of self-discovery, he has transformed life's challenges into a mission to inspire and uplift those ready to confront their fears and step into their power.

As a Quantum Healing Hypnosis Technique (QHHT) practitioner, Andrew has guided countless individuals through profound healing experiences, helping them uncover the root of their struggles and move toward lasting transformation. His podcast, Beyond Transcendence with Andrew, serves as a platform to explore personal growth, spirituality, and the stories of individuals who have overcome adversity.

Andrew's perspective on fear is deeply rooted in his life's journey. Growing up, he often battled self-doubt and uncertainty, but by facing his fears head-on, he discovered his purpose and the strength of resilience. He believes that fear, when understood, can be a powerful force for growth and healing—a belief that resonates throughout the pages of this book.

When he's not writing, podcasting, or guiding others through healing journeys, Andrew finds peace in nature, journaling, meditation, and creative outlets that nourish his soul. He is driven by the belief that every person holds the power to transform their lives, and he dedicates his work to empowering others on their paths of healing and self-discovery.

The Enemy Within: Fear as Our Greatest Opponent is Andrew's reflection on the power of confronting fear. In this book, he shares his lived experiences and some of the tools and insights he has gathered along the way. Andrew invites you to redefine fear—not as a roadblock but as a guide to a more meaningful and purposeful life.

www.ingramcontent.com/pod-product-compliance
Lightning Source LLC
Chambersburg PA
CBHW071221070526
44584CB00019B/3100